Daddy, Unbreak My Heart

Revived to Thrive

LaToya NaShae

3 He heals the broken hearted and binds up their wounds.

4 He counts the number of the stars; He calls them all by name.

Psalm 147:3-4

Dear One,

Healing is here... for you. The Lord calls out to you by name. Let down your walls and loosen your grip. Your heart has been fragmented for far too long. Trust in the Father as *your* Father. This is a relationship unlike what you have previously experienced. He will mend your broken pieces with a peace that surpasses all understanding. His is the love needed to revive your heart.

Father God, have Your way...

Sincerely,

LaToya NaShae

Table of Contents

The Journey Begins

Catch me! A little girl runs into her daddy's arms and is immediately hoisted to new heights. From here, she has a vantage point unlike that which her tiny frame offers. She looks low from on high as she rests in the security of her father's arms. But it all changes in an instant. His grip quickly loosens and, not having expected her daddy to fail her, she tumbles to the ground without being prepared for impact. *But you never drop me!* He walks away without an explanation or apology. *You never leave me!* Devastated, she is scarred both inside and out. Sure, her legs and arms are bruised from the jolt but more than anything, her fragile little heart is broken. *Why would my daddy hurt me? He is always supposed to catch me…* A whirlwind of emotions overtake her carefree nature.

Blocked? He blocked me?!?! Insecurities rush through her teen mind as yet another love connection disconnects. *Why don't my relationships ever work? What's wrong with me? I gave him everything he wanted and it still wasn't enough! Why am I not enough?* Absent is the trusted male perspective. Her dad isn't present to counsel or console. He never told her that you will lose the very thing you compromise to keep. Her mother instructed her on the ins and outs of womanhood, but her father's voice wasn't present to affirm her worth. His departure left her with a deficit. Now she sits broken with a heart full of unanswered questions.

Done. Done. And done! The life of this high achieving self-starter is marked by to-do lists, calculated risks, and insatiable ambition. *That partnership is MINE!* Blazing trails and climbing metaphorical ladders have proven profitable… and lonely. *My drive was birthed in isolation; isolation is now fuel to my focus.* Thus goes the rendition of her childhood from this hard-hearted professional. No time for friends or family; no time for love. After the unexpected death of her mother, her father wrapped himself even more tightly in the work of ministry. She wrapped herself in all things academic and athletic. One way or another, she would earn a full ride to a faraway university and separate herself from the fabricated Good News of her upbringing. She managed to succeed on every level without her parents or the God they served – the God who failed to protect and provide. She didn't need parents. She didn't need a limited Lord. *If God is love, I'm better off without Him. Love has never done a thing for me.*

No matter the age or gender, everyone knows the pain of rejection. It's hard to cope with being abandoned by someone who was always supposed to be there. How does one come to terms with being hurt by the one who should have been the protector? Everyone has experienced rejection, but this journey isn't for everyone. I am speaking to the hearts of ladies – young, old, and every age in between – who have had their hearts broken by the first man they ever loved...or ever wanted to love. This is for those who have constructed emotional walls to prevent themselves from being hurt to the same degree once again. To the strong and independent, the timid and co-dependent, the self-assured and the insecure, this journey is for you. It may not seem plausible that there is a God who will never leave nor forsake you, but lean in anyway. This journey is for you. To every woman who wears many masks to hide the pain caused by her father – the one who left or was never there, the one who did you harm rather than being a source of security – this is for you.

This journey is for those in need of healing. Yes, healing is available. Deliverance is possible. Freedom *is* an option. Your father failed you, but the Father never fails. His arms are stretched wide open to be the place of refuge, strength, peace, and love that you so desperately need.

No rejection. No disappointment. Affirmation and true

identity await you. His voice beckons you. Beautiful consistency and unending compassion that will mend the depths of your soul are in His presence. Yes, Abba Father, Daddy God, is able and willing to heal your brokenness. Hun, this journey is for you!

CHAPTER ONE

First Things First

Responding to Grace

⁸For by grace you are saved through faith; and not of yourselves: it is the gift of God; ⁹not of works, lest any man should boast. Ephesians 2:8-9, KJV

God loves you, yet doubt tries to have its way in your mind. The love of the Father is not extended because you're perfect. True, you haven't always served Him as you should. Still, He loves you. You are far from having mastered walking by faith and perhaps the light of your life is dim right now. He loves you. Quite possibly some unresolved issues have worked a wedge between you and your Creator. Maybe you *know* of Him but have yet to personally experience the power of His presence. You can't say that you know Him intimately. Even still, He loves you… just because.

We are conditioned to perform for approval. The

notion that God Almighty isn't checking for our perfection is crazy! Or is it? NEWSFLASH: It is not about what you have or have not done. What matters most is who you are – one fashioned in the likeness of His image, the very workmanship of His hands. You were made for a purpose – His purpose. You were created to be His daughter, His precious jewel. To be true, God wants you. How amazing is that! Your natural father rejected and neglected you, but the Father doesn't dare ignore you. His faithful promise is to never leave or forsake you. (See Genesis 28:15). The love of God isn't earned, only received. He loves beyond emotions. His love is thorough, perfect, unconditional, and without limits. It is with that love that He invites you into His family, making you a child of the Most High by way of salvation. The price was paid by Christ. Will you receive the gift?

Grace allows you to experience the goodness of God at the expense of Christ's sacrifice. By grace you are saved through faith. That statement is only as powerful in your life as the depth of your understanding.

[6] For when we were still without strength, in due time Christ died for the ungodly. [7] For scarcely for a righteous man will one die; yet perhaps for a good man someone would even dare to die. [8] But God demonstrates His own love toward us, in that while we were still sinners, Christ died for us. [9] Much

more then, having now been justified by His Blood, we shall be saved from wrath through Him. Romans 5:6-9

Justified. You are made guiltless by the Blood of Jesus. In Him you are not just snatched from the enemy's grip and offered eternal life. With His presence comes an anointing – the very anointing of Jesus, the Messiah – that is capable of breaking every yoke and healing every pain. Yes, He can heal your deepest hurts if only you will accept Him as your personal Savior and Lord.

[16] For God so loved the world, that He gave His only begotten Son, that whoever believes in Him should not perish but have everlasting life. [17] For God did not send His Son into the world to condemn the world, but the world through Him might be saved. John 3:16-17

Who needs salvation? Everybody! No one is capable of living righteously enough to meet God's standard. *For all have sinned and fall short of the glory of God.* (Romans 3:23). Without the Blood, we miss the mark. Our greatest efforts to be good are not good enough without the Holy Spirit's seal of approval. We cannot please the Lord in our strength. Our strength is not what He is after. Praise Jesus! Faith pleases the Lord. By faith, we receive Him. By faith we experience a life of wholeness and victory. Perfect? No.

Righteous? Absolutely! In Christ, we are the righteousness of God. (II Corinthians 5:21).

⁸ But what does it say? "The word is near you, in your mouth and in your heart" (that is, the word of faith which we preach): ⁹ that if you confess with your mouth the Lord Jesus and believe in your heart that God has raised Him from the dead, you will be saved. Romans 10:8-9

You are saved *by* grace *through* faith. You are saved from this world's unfruitful systems, brokenness, bondage and most importantly, from an eternity of separation from the Father. Your confidence in knowing Jesus conquered death, hell and the grave to rise victoriously on your behalf and the willingness to reverence Him as Lord rightly positions you to receive salvation. You have the faith, correct? Then open your mouth to receive. *Confession is made unto salvation.* (Romans 10:10). It's this simple: confess with your mouth and believe in your heart. Jesus died to become Savior; He now reigns as Lord. To know God as Father, you must first know His Son as Lord.

The Lord isn't really being slow about his promise, as some people think. No, he is being patient for your sake. He does not want anyone to be destroyed, but wants everyone to repent. II Peter 3:9, NLT

Salvation is God's will for every man, woman, boy, and girl. He gave His Son so that whoever – meaning *all* are eligible – believes in Christ shall be saved. That's you, boo! Believe. Rely on Him, trust in Him, accept Him, and allow His Spirit to live through you. Just as the pain of your past was not God's plan for you neither is condemnation. That which the enemy meant for your destruction will be used by God to build your testimony. Trust Him enough to put your life in His hands. The first step toward receiving emotional healing is to receive the ultimate healing: salvation.

If you have yet to accept Christ as your personal Savior and Lord and you are ready to surrender your life so that healing can begin, recite this prayer to receive Him into your heart.

Father,

I understand my need for You far surpasses anything capable of being supplied by another person. To know You more deeply and more personally is what I need. Thank You for being patient. Thank You for paving the way for me to abide in Your presence. Your love is calling; I am responding with a repentant and surrendered heart. I believe that Jesus died and rose again for the cleansing of my sins.

I receive You, Jesus, as Lord and Savior. By Your Blood I am made right. Jesus, because You live, I am redeemed. At this moment my heart is being renewed. By faith, I believe that new life is in You. Lead me by Your Spirit. Teach me to live righteously before You. My life is now Yours. Your will be done. In Jesus' name I pray. Amen.

First Things First: Thoughts of Revival

Your heart is made new; yet, life is the same. With time your inward transformation will shift the landscape of your outer existence. Relax. Newness is a process. Until then, write the vision and make it plain. Describe in detail how you envision the healed and whole version of you.

CHAPTER TWO

Acceptance

Royal Adoption

1 Therefore being justified by faith, we have peace with God through our Lord Jesus Christ: 2 by whom also we have access by faith into this grace wherein we stand, and rejoice in the hope of the glory of God. Romans 5:1-2

You are justified. You are made right in the eyes of God. Let that sink in. The Blood of Jesus has cleansed you from all unrighteousness, bringing you into right-standing with God and granting you access to undeserved privilege. Believe and receive your position by faith. Hun, are now a child of the King!

Let these truths take root in your spirit. You are sooo far from a mistake! You are loved. You were created on purpose for a purpose. Regardless of the lies Satan has tried to force-feed you, you are not a reject. Neither are you a misfit or an outcast. God handcrafted you to be counted among His children. At the point of salvation, you became royalty. Come through, roy-al-tee!

14 For as many as are led by the Spirit of God, these are sons of God. 15 For you did not receive the spirit of bondage again to fear, but you received the Spirit of adoption by whom we cry out, "Abba, Father." 16 The Spirit Himself bears witness with our spirit that we are children of God. Romans 8:14-16

The Spirit of God now dwells in you as a comfort and guide. This isn't about bondage. It definitely isn't demonic possession. Unlike the enemy, God's intent is not to puppet you. He has sent His Holy Spirit to indwell you as a source of empowerment. For so long you have been pushed by people and persuaded by negative emotions. This is different. The Spirit leads; you follow. Life has been a roller coaster of trial and error episodes. This is so different. You see, *the steps of a good [woman] are ordered by the Lord: and He delights in [her] way.* (Psalm 37:23). The Holy Spirit directs you according to His perfect plan for your life. It is His will for peace to rule in your heart; it is His desire for your life to be characterized by wholeness. God is not far off and distant, ruling with an iron fist. No ma'am! He is up close and personal, causing His Word to be fulfilled on your behalf. That's the way of your oh-so-divine Dad.

Know that He has seen every tear and heard each plea. The Lord your God is well aware of the emotional scars that have led to the barricading of your heart. Believe me; He knows. You are in need of healing.

Healing begins with understanding in your heart and mind that you are accepted. Accepted? Yes. He chose not to knock down the door of your heart's entry. No, He waited patiently to be invited. All the while He was there with open arms, ready to make you His.

The Father loves you beyond measure. You can't even wrap your mind around that thought, I'm sure. Prepare to have your mind blown. Wait for it...God loves you as much as He loves Jesus! Whew! I know. That's a weighty standpoint. Take time to process it. Everything that Jesus is entitled to – without exception – is granted to you as well. Don't take my word for it. Your proof is in the Word.

And if children, then heirs—heirs of God and joint heirs with Christ, if indeed we suffer with Him, that we may also be glorified together. Romans 8:17

By the precious Blood of Christ you have been made OFFICIAL. You are an heir of God and joint-heir with Christ. Your Daddy loves you and like any good father, He is willing to provide for your every need. Unlike any other father, this Father has the ability to meet every need, naturally and spiritually. God will move heaven and earth on the behalf of His children. My dear, the earth will shake for you!

⁶ In my distress I called upon the Lord, and cried out to my God; He heard my voice from His temple, and my cry came before Him, even to His ears. ⁷ Then the earth shook and trembled; the foundations of the hills also quaked and were shaken, because He was angry, ⁸ smoke went up from His nostrils, and devouring fire from His mouth; coals were kindled by it. ⁹ He bowed the heavens also, and came down with darkness under His feet. Psalm 18:6-9

Christ has defeated Satan to ensure your freedom. Be mindful not to forget that God is the same yesterday, today, and forevermore. He will defy the odds and cast down demons for you! Every battle you encounter is the Lord's. Stand. The kingdom of darkness is under His feet and yours as well. The separation between you and the enemy's forces is your faith in God's Word. When attacks attempt to steal your peace, cry out to God. He doesn't take assaults against His babies lightly. Declare His Word with the authority that has been granted to you. Put all confidence in His faithfulness. *And I will give you the keys of the kingdom of heaven, and whatever you bind on earth will be bound in heaven, and whatever you loose on earth will be loosed in heaven.* (Matthew 16:19). The keys are yours. Activate them by faith in knowing that God will move heaven and earth just for you, His daughter.

Lord of All Creation,

That title carries immeasurable weight and authority. Still, You choose to make Yourself accessible. Thank You for adopting this precious soul into Your family. You haven't chosen her as a distant relative; You call her daughter. She is Yours.

As You look on her with love and affection, reassure her of who she is in You. Remind her that she is fearfully and wonderfully made. Lord, I pray that You would bind the insecurities that plague her mind. They are contrary to Your word and have no right to trouble her heart.

Thank You for the newness of life offered by Your Spirit. Continue to fill her with fresh revelation of what it means to have a personal walk with You. Help her to become confident in discerning and following Your voice. You are the Father that never fails. We give You unending praise with our mouths, unwavering commitment in our walk, and absolute devotion from our hearts. You are worthy of all this and more. Thank You, Lord, for the work You are doing in Your daughter's life. Continue to minister to the depths of her heart. Heal. Deliver. Restore. It is Your will for chains to be broken and yokes to be destroyed. You will complete the work of healing You started in her heart. We are grateful for Your faithfulness. In Jesus' name we pray. Amen.

Acceptance: Thoughts of Revival

Acceptance has a formal definition but let's drop the formalities, shall we? You have been adopted by the King of kings. What does being accepted into the kingdom of God as a daughter mean to you?

Called to Rejection

LaToya NaShae

Want to know what I've learned about roles? I have learned that we sometimes make them too constraining. Attached to roles are expectations and, unfortunately, expectations are not always met. FACT: Falling short is a facet of the human condition. Realize it or not, expectations are up against the opposing forces of personal limitations and free will. Expectations set a standard, but standards aren't always lived up to. Decisions are made. Distance is felt. Time causes a hand full of memories to fade. Questions go unanswered. And hurt feelings mature into a root of rejection that bares fruit not fit for consumption. Thankfully, pain doesn't have the final say, at least not for those who are in Christ.

I am number three of four. I cannot and will not attempt to speak on behalf of my siblings. We four have the same father but different mothers. We grew up in separate households with experiences as unique as we are individuals. Even the shared experience of losing our father was felt differently. For me, it initially wasn't felt at all. He passed away two months shy of my eleventh birthday. I opted to go to school rather than attend his funeral, a decision for which I still have no regrets.

Back then, my heart was most likely too young and too unbothered to be hardened. I had no rhyme or reason for saying goodbye to someone with whom I shared so very few hellos. I appreciate my mom's willingness and wisdom in allowing me to choose. I chose to continue on with life as usual.

My father passed away; my dad lived on. Confused? Let me explain. My parents married in November of 1989. My dad – the one who stepped in after my father stepped away – was the man I unknowingly needed. He calls me one of his greatest blessings, and I share the same sentiment in regards to him. My dad has been a consistent source of natural security, stability, and strength for nearly my entire life. As much of a protector and provider as he has been, there was no protecting me from realizing there was one who provided half of my DNA, yet chose not to own his role in my life.

Wisdom is the principal thing; therefore, get wisdom. And in all your getting, get understanding. Proverbs 4:7

I now understand that roles create constraining expectations and if our expectations are not met, our wholeness (or lack thereof) bears the burden. It took three years for me to feel anything. Three years after my father's death, tears fell. Loss was felt. My pain wasn't tied to losing my father but rather losing the opportunity to get understanding. With questions comes the expectation of answers. Unfortunately, my questions had no choice but to remain unanswered. My heart wanted to know why – why not visit or call or attend school functions? Why not verbalize the reason for your absence? Did you love me? With each question, rejection plotted to have its way.

It is assumed that girls with daddy issues behave in a certain manner. However, promiscuity wasn't my plight because "daddy issues" were not my real problem. Remember, I *had* a dad who was present. He believed in candid conversations, ensuring that I knew my worth and the intricacies of the games some men play. Nope. I didn't have daddy issues in the general sense; I had answer issues. Because my father wasn't alive to provide answers, I became the answer. Problem-solving, performance, and perfectionism became my addiction. I mapped out my life and set the wheels in motion. The goal was to be a successful, self-sufficient self-starter so as not to depend on others to play their role. No dependency, no disappointment, right? Me, myself, and I had it all figured out. It is interesting that ambition is only as healthy as its origin. In an attempt to blaze my own trail, I failed to take God's will for my life into consideration.

9 The heart is the most deceitful thing there is and desperately wicked. No one can really know how bad it is! 10 Only the Lord knows! He searches all hearts and examines deepest motives so he can give to each person his right reward, according to his deeds—how he has lived.
Jeremiah 17:9-10, TLB

Wisdom is to rightly apply and live out the Word of God. As His Word is expressed through the posture of our hearts, the content of our thoughts, and the righteousness of our words, understanding unfolds. The Word came alive for me at the age of sixteen. I began to find my true identity in the book of Romans; I heard the voice of God with absolute clarity. He began to order my steps. Little did I know He had been ordering them all along. The Lord our God specializes in transforming ashes into beauty and hurt into healing. Redemption is real, y'all! He used the jumbled mess of my unanswered questions to craft an answer for those bound by rejection. The more I came to understand WHOSE I am, the more it became clear that my plan for self-promotion did not serve His purpose. In His presence, all things – good and bad – work together to produce His good pleasure in the lives of those who love Him as Lord. (See Romans 8:28).

And they overcame him by the blood of the Lamb and by the word of their testimony, and they did not love their lives to the death. Revelation 12:11

I now understand that healing is a process, and every process has a path and pace. Slowly, steadily, surely, healing comes to those with surrendered hearts. The process of my healing went from indifference to anger, then numbness to feeling, from feeling to awareness, and now healing is here. Feeling came while writing the first edition of *Daddy, Unbreak My Heart*. I thought I was healed until tears began to flow. Numbness was preventing the healing and wholeness that comes as a result of abiding with an unveiled face in the presence of the Father.

I buried feelings of rejection, but what happens to a buried seed? Ignoring issues gives them opportunity to take root, bloom, and bear fruit. That fruit caused the weight of performance to rest on my shoulders. Before I understood my identity as a daughter of the King, I made it my responsibility to create an identity founded in scholastic excellence and the pursuit of prestige. *Unbreak* broke me to rebuild me. It was the painful yet necessary reminder that I am incapable of healing me. As the Lord lovingly uncovered my unanswered questions, He began to answer questions I never knew to ask.

Before I formed you, I knew you. No twist or turn of your life has caught Me off guard. I allowed you to feel rejection without being destroyed by it. I will never completely remove the pain of rejection. As long as you can feel it, you can relate.

With that revelation, understanding came…

[88] Revive me according to Your lovingkindness, so that I may keep the testimony of Your mouth. [89] Forever, O LORD, Your word is settled in heaven. [90] Your faithfulness endures to all generations; You established the earth, and it abides. Psalm 119:88-90

Once upon a time I had a disdain for dependence. Now, I desire dependence on the One who created everything by speaking to nothing. Before I knew rejection's sting, the Lord knew me. He knew the plan and path necessary for His purpose to be fulfilled. I rest in the One who satisfies with honey from a rock – my heavenly Father. He is the One who ushers in healing to remedy life's hurts. In all my getting of understanding, I now see living through the redemption of rejection was crucial to the call on my life. To equip others to live like they know WHOSE they are, I had to become fully persuaded that there is One who will never run from His role. He endured rejection for the benefit of my healing. His love mended the broken pieces of my heart. I now live to lead others to His love, because His love will always fulfill its role.

³ He is despised and rejected by men, a Man of sorrows and acquainted with grief. And we hid, as it were, our faces from Him; He was despised, and we did not esteem Him.
⁴ Surely He has borne our griefs and carried our sorrows; yet we esteemed Him stricken, smitten by God, and afflicted.
⁵ But He was wounded for our transgressions, He was bruised for our iniquities; the chastisement for our peace was upon Him, and by His stripes we are healed.
Isaiah 53:3-5

CHAPTER THREE

Voices

Reverse of the Curse

[5] *"Look, I am sending you the prophet Elijah before the great and dreadful day of the Lord arrives. [6] His preaching will turn the hearts of fathers to their children, and the hearts of children to their fathers. Otherwise, I will come and strike the land with a curse."* Malachi 4:5-6, NLT

It is what it is! But what if what it is has not been rightly defined? If allowed, presumptuous voices will dictate your identity. When you lack revelation of who you are, they fill in the blanks. Labels are placed based on deficits. Voids are evaluated, and opinions are inserted. Voices pull from current circumstances and generational trends to determine who you are and where you are going. Stereotypes become synonyms. Statistics state your limits. Some might even attempt to use Scripture to crucify your value. True, curses creep in when fathers are absent. However, paternal presence does not guarantee protective covering. (Love is the "It Factor," but we'll get to that later.) Not every father knows the power of his voice because not every father knows his worth. By the weight of a father's words, identity is decreed. But what about when he doesn't know who he is? A father's absence or silence or lack of understanding creates space for other voices to have their say.

[16] Then they journeyed from Bethel. And when there was but a little distance to go to Ephrath, Rachel labored in childbirth, and she had hard labor. [17] Now it came to pass, when she was in hard labor, that the midwife said to her, "Do not fear; you will have this son also." [18] And so it was, as her soul was departing (for she died), that she called his name Ben-Oni; but his father called him Benjamin. Genesis 35:16-18

With her last breath, Rachel named her baby boy Ben-Oni. Jacob wasn't having it! He replaced "son of my sorrow" with Benjamin, meaning son of my right hand. He reversed the curse by trading sorrow for joy. The father stepped in to pronounce a blessing where a contradicting voice declared a curse. How much more can your heavenly Father do for you??? Before you were formed in your mother's womb, He knew you… He spoke blessings over you. Voices have tried to mute The Voice that created everything by speaking to nothing, but greater is He who watches over you! No negative word spoken against you shall prosper. Lack cannot forever limit you. Even now, the Son is seated at the right hand of the Father. Together they are speaking to every one of your life's voids.

[31] What then shall we say to these things? If God is for us, who can be against us? [32] He who did not spare His own Son, but delivered Him up for us all, how shall He not with Him also freely give us all things? [33] Who shall bring a charge against God's elect? It is God who justifies. [34] Who is he who condemns? It is Christ who died, and furthermore is also risen, who is even at the right hand of God, who also makes intercession for us. Romans 8:31-34

Be of good cheer, the Father covers you. Count it all joy, His love made a way for you. Pay no mind to the voices. Every tongue that rises against you shall be condemned. (Isaiah 54:17). The voices have no power over the Word! Remember the Risen One and the Word are one. In the beginning was the Word, and the Word lovingly calls you by name.

Praise be unto God who fills in the cracks of every unfilled role. It is written, "When my father and mother forsake me, the Lord will take care of me." (Psalm 27:10). With lots of facts and very little faith, unauthorized voices attempt to predict your destiny. They dare to weigh down who you are based on what you don't have. Thankfully, there is One who supplies all your needs by the integrity of His name. Jehovah Jireh, the Lord who provides, is committed to providing for you.

But now, O Jacob, listen to the Lord who created you. O Israel, the one who formed you says, "Do not be afraid, for I have ransomed you. I have called you by name; you are mine. Isaiah 43:1, NLT

¹ Say there! Is anyone thirsty? Come and drink—even if you have no money! Come, take your choice of wine and milk— it's all free! ² Why spend your money on food that doesn't give you strength? Why pay for groceries that do you no good? Listen and I'll tell you where to get good food that fattens up the soul!
³ Come to me with your ears wide open. Listen, for the life of your soul is at stake. I am ready to make an everlasting covenant with you, to give you all the unfailing mercies and love that I had for King David. Isaiah 55:1-3, NLT

Lean in, hun. Turn your heart to the Father. Listen to the One who created you. Press into the presence of the Lord God Almighty. Rest. Be assured that He has ransomed you. Naysayers say otherwise, but Love has lifted you from the cursed place. No longer a child of sorrow, you are the daughter of His right hand. From the abundance of His heart, the Lord speaks your name. He proclaims a hopeful future and a bright destiny. The voice of your Father defines you. You are who He says you are! You are accepted. You are favored. You are loved.

Most Precious Heavenly Father,

With grateful hearts, we thank You. The voices fall silent as heaven's reality is brought to earth. I thank You for this daughter's revelation of who she is in You. Today, she is set free from hindering labels. Gone are the oppressive chains that bind her to a restrictive identity. In You she is free and healed and whole. Strengthen her to walk in the newness of her God-identity. In Jesus' name we pray. Amen.

Voices: Thoughts of Revival

What passage of Scripture most personally affirms who God says you are? Explain.

CHAPTER FOUR

Bag Daddy

Commissioning the Grief Carrier

³ He is despised and rejected by men, a Man of sorrows and acquainted with grief. And we hid, as it were, our faces from Him; He was despised, and we did not esteem Him.
⁴ Surely He has borne our griefs and carried our sorrows; yet we esteemed Him stricken, smitten by God, and afflicted.
Isaiah 53:3-4

Rejection is a universal experience with varying degrees; no one is exempt. Its sting is felt by all – even the Son of God. Say what? Yes, hun-neey! We know Jesus was wounded for our transgressions and bruised for our iniquities. We are mindful to remember that our healing is in His stripes. Lord, we thank You for the price paid on our behalf - included in that cost was the burden of our emotional trauma. Friend, when was the last time you paused to ponder that Christ bore your griefs and sorrows as well? Brace yourself. It's about to get real.

You know your story better than I do. Maybe you remember being abandoned by your father, or it could be that his identity remains a mystery. Perhaps he was a predator who taught you to fear a man's touch. Is the issue that your dad was physically present yet emotionally unavailable? Whatever the case may be, your past is as concrete as it is real. There is no changing it. Because you remember, you also feel. Thankfully, being able to feel does nothing to disqualify you from healing.

Rejection's roots run deep, and its fruit is a force to be reckoned with. Distrust, bitterness, pride, manipulation – the list of reject fruit is unending. Rather than falling by the wayside, this resentment-filled produce becomes baggage. In the absence of a resolve to get healed, we become bag ladies.

Bag lady you gone hurt your back,

dragging all them bags like that

I guess nobody ever told you

All you must hold onto, is you, is you, is you

Bag Lady by Erykah Badu

Ms. Badu had me humming along until that last line. All you must hold onto is you? Solace has never been found in me hugging me. When painful memories invade my space, I don't turn to social media as my digital diary. Posting for likes and double taps won't get the job done. What's craved most is the peace that passes all understanding. I need a word, a worship song – SOMETHING – to help me feel the Father's nearness. To cling to the Great One is to embrace a love so perfect and powerful that it drives out all forms of darkness.

How precious is Your lovingkindness, O God! Therefore the children of men put their trust under the shadow of Your wings. Psalm 36:7

The past cannot be erased; however, the fruit of rejection can be permanently discarded. Decay and distress have no place in your destiny. You are called and chosen and consecrated for divine turnaround. The God of the gaps is ready to place distance between you and your promise-blockers. Wait. What's this about promise-blockers? We're talking about healing from rejection. The hard truth is this: Rejection's fruit is primarily eaten by the rejected. Anger hinders you. Unforgiveness hardens your heart. Seeking revenge positions you to sow seeds that will yield a self-destructive crop. Self-sufficiency causes you to miss the beauty of relationships. While heartbreak was not your choice, healing is. Hun, you have to be an active participant in your deliverance. Otherwise, a toxic harvest will overtake you.

⁷ Do not be deceived, God is not mocked; for whatever a man sows, that he will also reap. ⁸ For he who sows to his flesh will of the flesh reap corruption, but he who sows to the Spirit will of the Spirit reap everlasting life. Galatians 6:7-8

Be bold. Be brave. Be willing to hand over your baggage. Unclench your nails from the pain you angrily grip. Dump the stockpile of offenses that weigh down your heart. Unbind your mind from thoughts of unforgiveness and revenge. There is a Grief Carrier waiting to carry your load. Christ was smitten and stricken and afflicted for you. He is qualified to bear your burdens.

Will the memories go away? I doubt it. Will old feelings occasionally stir? Yes, that is likely. Then what's the point?!?! The difference is that pain will no longer rule your heart. You will no longer be a worshiper of hurt. The past won't be your jailor. A new perspective will allow you to see that what happened to you does not have the authority to define you. Your heart will be lighter and your soul at peace as a result of allowing Bag Daddy to have His way.

²⁵ "'Then it will be as though I had sprinkled clean water on you, for you will be clean—your filthiness will be washed away, your idol worship gone. ²⁶ And I will give you a new heart—I will give you new and right desires—and put a new spirit within you. I will take out your stony hearts of sin and give you new hearts of love. Ezekiel 36:25-26, TLB

Father,

Pull Your daughter closer. Take her deeper into the shadow of Your wings. Help her to breathe. Exhale chaos; inhale peace. Exhale baggage and bondage; inhale the sweet freedom of surrender. Assure her that healing is here... if only she will receive it.

Every knee shall bow at the name of Jesus. (Philippians 2:10). It's time for your pain to fall to its knees. Name every pain that needs to bow, and then counter these with the Word of God. Find at least one verse per pain point so that your prayers for healing are backed by God's truth.

Relentless Love

Mariette

Intentional numbness is to deprive one's self of feeling or responsiveness. I inadvertently chose numbness as a coping mechanism. Let me be honest. Feeling is frightening, so I spent years being numb – unable to receive love from my mother, father, or anyone else around me. An impenetrable wall of non-feelings barricaded my heart serving as a blockade even between the Lord and me. Little did I know the remedy for my heart's hardness was rooted and grounded in forgiveness.

This is what the LORD *says to the people of Judah and to Jerusalem: "Break up your unplowed ground and do not sow among thorns.* Jeremiah 4:3, NIV

Resiliency became my thorny badge of honor. Externally, my bounce back game was official. Internally, feigned resiliency was killing me softly. I have accomplished much despite a broken childhood. Rejection wrapped itself around my identity early in life as a paralyzing accident left me positioned as my mother's primary caregiver. It squeezed more tightly every time I felt as though her wants were placed over my needs. Nurturing fell by the wayside. Affirmation wasn't a thing. My mother's health took precedence over my emotional wellbeing. I kicked performance into high gear. Although I had accepted Christ as Savior before my mother's accident, I lacked understanding of the depth of His sacrifice. I didn't get that He died for me; it didn't click that He chose my life over His. A determination to prove that I was enough was the fruit that rejection produced in my life. I had to prove I was enough to be loved and chosen by my mother. I needed to prove I was enough for my dad to remain present.

Circumcise yourselves to the Lord, circumcise your hearts, you people of Judah and inhabitants of Jerusalem. Jeremiah 4:4, NIV

I remember my dad dumping my mother's clothes on my grandmother's front lawn and driving away. I remember three year old me attempting to help my mom gather her clothes before they became rain soaked. This was my introduction to my father's absence… and a calloused heart. Enter numbness. He reappeared for my fifth birthday. I distinctly remember the maroon sweat suit and Mickey

Mouse purse he brought as gifts. Gone again. My dad popped up five years later with a new family. I had a little brother and step siblings now. This solidified numbness and the notion that I was not enough.

I hid behind education and accomplishments. The power of perceived perfection became intoxicating. No one would have known I didn't have it all together because they weren't allowed to get close enough to see the cracks in my façade. Over time, self-preservation taught me to survey the landscape of my past and piece together the fragmented parts. A life could be built from the tattered remains. *I could make this work. I was fully capable to pulling it all together.*

I rearranged feelings of rejection to make amends with my father. He was open to answering hard questions and I was open to allowing him in my life. Meanwhile, I had to combat my mother's jealousy. There I was wedged in the middle again. Anger welled up inside me. This was NOT how it was supposed to be. They should have been my covering and protection. Instead, I was left as a wide open target for the enemy's fiery darts. My anger extended to God for not shielding me from their shortcomings.

I pressed on. Disappointment, rejection, neglect, and feeling unloved became my norm. Exceedingly, abundantly weren't within the scope of my expectation. I did my best to play the hand I was dealt. That is so unbiblical, I know. This was so not the abundant life God promised but honestly, I didn't think that promise pertained to me. The kill, steal, and destroy part seemed more applicable.

The thief does not come except to steal, and to kill, and to destroy. I have come that they may have life, and that they may have it more abundantly. John 10:10

Unbeknownst to me, Christ was in relentless pursuit of my shattered heart. I Corinthians 13 starts with, "Love is patient. Love is kind." I never thought to open my heart to receive God's perfect love because all other love had failed. Everyone close to me always let me down. There were times when I wasn't sure if God was for me or against me, because the pain in my life screamed louder than His voice. He was patient and persistent until I was able to hear.

The Lord used *Daddy, Unbreak My Heart* to break up the fallow ground of my soul. It was the vehicle that carried me to healing. With the turn of every page, God spoke to the core of my being. Healing was initiated! Like a skillful surgeon, He began to dig out the death and decay of deceit planted by the enemy. He assured my wounded heart that His love for me was unconditional. He just didn't tell me once or twice. No, I was constantly reminded of how much my heavenly Father cared for me. Even when I tried retreating behind the comfort of my isolating wall, Love called out to me. He answered my questions and endured my fiery anger. That's longsuffering, indeed. The Lord never gave up on me. His faithful consistency continues delivering illuminating healing to the dark places of my heart. My heart now knows well that love is patient and kind.

I have accepted the Blood of Jesus as enough to make me enough. The Blood gave me the strength to forgive my mom for her mistakes and the man who shot her. Grace empowered me to release the anger associated with my dad's absence. Revelation of God's mercy towards me has served as enough for me to let go of negative thoughts toward family members who I once felt could have done more. The blood of Jesus and His all-encompassing love are enough for my past, present, and future.

Oh, the overwhelming, never-ending,

reckless love of God

Oh, it chases me down, fights 'til I'm found,

leaves the ninety-nine

Reckless Love by Cory Asbury

As I continue this journey of healing, I am assured that God will never leave nor forsake me. Because His perfect love casts out all fear, I will not forget that I am never alone. Even on the days when I am most afraid to move forward, the Spirit of the Lord is with me. Numbness is no longer my normal. I know that I am accepted and loved even when feelings try to convince me otherwise. I have been adopted into the body of Christ. His Blood is truly enough.

About Mariette

Mariette is a wife, minister, civic-minded leader and more. This Elkton, Kentucky native currently resides in Cincinnati, Ohio where she serves as the executive director of an early childhood education program. Together, she and her husband, Frank, serve as the founders and lead pastors of First Response Community Church, an outreach ministry for the homeless, elderly, and incarcerated.

CHAPTER FIVE

SET APART FOR PURPOSE

Dare to Shine

[14] I have given them Your word; and the world has hated them because they are not of the world, just as I am not of the world. [15] I do not pray that You should take them out of the world, but that You should keep them from the evil one. [16] They are not of the world, just as I am not of the world. [17] Sanctify them by Your truth. Your word is truth. [18] As You sent Me into the world, I also have sent them into the world. [19] And for their sakes I sanctify Myself, that they also may be sanctified by the truth. John 17:14-19

The Word of God embedded in your heart and at work in your life sets you apart from the crowd. You aren't the norm. You are among a chosen generation, counted as one of His special people who are called to proclaim His praises, one whom He led out of darkness and encompassed with His marvelous light. (See I Peter 2:9). His Word sanctifies you. Yes, you are different. The chasm between you and the world is the mark of distinction placed on your life by the Holy Spirit's presence. You are different– and divinely so.

I do not pray that You should take them out of the world, but that You should keep them from the evil one. John 17:15

You have work to do. Your life – an ever-evolving tale of triumphs and trials – is a story that testifies of the grace and faithfulness of God. Just as Jesus prayed for His disciples in days of old, He also prays for you. At this very instant Christ, your Savior and Redeemer, is seated at the right hand of the Father interceding on your behalf. Imagine what He might be saying.

She is not of the world; however, the world needs her light. Keep her from the evil one. Sanctify and strengthen her by the power of the Holy Spirit. Father, use her for Your glory.

My dear, God doesn't have to be coerced. He can use you. He *wants* to use you. Like the declaration of II Corinthians 4:8-9, you have been hard-pressed on every side, but yet you are not crushed; you have been perplexed, but you are not in utter despair; you've known persecution, but by no means have you been forsaken by the Holy One of heaven; you have been struck down, but today you stand, not having been destroyed. Your testimony is the story of an overcomer. You have been hurt, neglected, and rejected; still you press forward. Let these words resonate in your heart:

6 For God, who said, "Let there be light in the darkness," has made this light shine in our hearts so we could know the glory of God that is seen in the face of Jesus Christ.
7 We now have this light shining in our hearts, but we ourselves are like fragile clay jars containing this great treasure. This makes it clear that our great power is from God, not from ourselves. II Corinthians 4:6-7, New Living Translation

You are now free from the pressure to be strong in your own might. I know all too well what it is like to be in self-preservation mode. Open your eyes. The root of that is fear. Your heart says, "No one else is going to get the chance to hurt me." You have constructed wall after wall of defence mechanisms, but doing so is no longer necessary. Within you is a great treasure; those walls have to be brought down for that treasure to be revealed.

As You sent Me into the world, I also have sent them into the world. (John 17:18). You have been given the Word and set apart for God's good purpose. That purpose is to be a light in darkness. The aim isn't to send you into the world so that it can devour you. Instead, the world will be made better because of the excellent power of God seen *through* you. Chains are broken and the enemy is defeated by the Blood of the Lamb and the words of our testimonies (Revelation 12:11). Your testimony will destroy yokes if only you will refuse to remain silent.

13 "You are the salt of the earth; but if the salt loses its flavor, how shall it be seasoned? It is then good for nothing but to be thrown out and trampled underfoot by men. 14 "You are the light of the world. A city that is set on a hill cannot be hidden. 15 Nor do they light a lamp and put it under a basket, but on a lampstand, and it gives light to all who are in the house. Matthew 5:13-15

Although not every situation is caused by God, everything you have gone through can be used for His glory. Don't allow your pain to be in vain. God has preserved you all these years for a purpose that exceeds self. Others need your salt; they need your light. There are young ladies who need to know that you made it. Your dad wasn't the father he should have been, but your Father never removed His hand from your life. You are that city on a hill. You are that lamp. Don't hide from fear that transparency equates to weakness. No, my dear, even in weakness you are made strong in the Lord. (See II Corinthians 12:9). His grace is sufficient to handle to your brokenness. The light of Christ is able to shine through your cracked places. Trust Him to heal you but don't stop there. Be the catalyst that prompts others to seek Him for healing as well. Be strong in the Lord and of good courage. Let your light shine.

Lord,

No love compares to Yours. No one is as faithful, consistent, patient, or genuine as You. Thank You, heavenly Father, just for being who You are.

As this daughter of Yours continues to approach Your throne with holy boldness and hunger, continue to reveal Yourself to her. As she walks in deeper understanding of who You are, she will come to know who she is in You. You made no mistakes when creating her. Life has hurt her, but You have always loved her. Wrap her in Your love. Holy Spirit, minister to her heart. Stir up the gift that has been placed inside of her. Light her path, O God. She is a vessel for Your use; may every aspect of her life glorify You. Lead her in the way of hope and true fulfillment. Place a hedge of protection around her as You strengthen her to push back against the enemy's forces. May she follow after Your voice as a sheep follows its shepherd. Give her lion-like courage that is motivated by her trust in Your Word. There is no variation in who You are. Help her to know and rest in this truth.

You are Jehovah-Rohi, her Shepherd. Jehovaha-Rophe, her healer. Jehovah-M'Kaddesh, her sanctifier. Jehovah-Tsori, her strength. Jehovah-Magen, her shield. You are the source and supplier of Your daughter's every need. May her heart swell with devotion for You. In the name of Jesus, Lord, let Your perfect will be done in her life. Amen.

Set Apart for Purpose: Thoughts of Revival

It's true, you know? Everything that God does He does with purpose in mind. That includes creating you. How might God use your story to accomplish His will on earth?

CHAPTER SIX

Release Therapy

Freedom in Forgiveness
Do not be overcome by evil, but overcome evil with good.
Romans 12:21

The memories of abuse are still painfully real. Your tears have been far too many to count. You have become quite acquainted with the frustration and confusion of rejection. Physical and emotional scars continue to make their presence known. Still, healing is here. Your spirit has taken some mighty blows. As much as you want to be a faith giant, fear holds you back. Trust? You want to trust, but you aren't sure how to trust and protect your heart at the same time. Healing is here. Your desire is to move forward but your past continues pulling you back. You desperately want your heart to be mended. You cry out, "Dear God, help me to forget!" But His still small voice whispers back that both your healing and freedom lie in forgiveness. This again? Yep.

⁹ In this manner, therefore, pray: Our Father in heaven, hallowed be Your name. ¹⁰ Your kingdom come. Your will be done on earth as it is in heaven. ¹¹ Give us this day our daily bread. ¹² And forgive us our debts, as we forgive our debtors. ¹³ And do not lead us into temptation, but deliver us from the evil one. For Yours is the kingdom and the power and the glory forever. Amen. Matthew 6:9-13

The Holy One of Heaven who does all things for His name's sake wants to make heaven's reality *your* reality. As your loving Father, He desires to fulfill the desires of your heart. He is well able to meet your daily needs and go far beyond your wildest dreams. He *wants* to do these things for you. The Lord wants to shower down mercy and grace, alleviating burdens you may rightfully deserve to bear and blessing you with divine treasures beyond your imagination. The Blood makes it possible. Forgiveness positions you for endless possibilities.

Remember Whose you are. With each new day comes the opportunity to become more and more like Jesus. Transformation does not occur without stretching beyond the borders of familiarity. (I heard you sigh. Don't feel bad. I did too!) Now is the time for you to extend mercy just as mercy has been extended to you. You're hesitant. I get it. You have known hurt longer than you've known healing. Pain is...

familiar. Can I challenge a bit? Consider this: Comfort zones aren't necessarily comfortable; they're just what you know. Dysfunction can either be embraced or released. Boo, healing is in the release. The Father is strengthening you to shake loose from bitterness and rage. He is serving an eviction notice to the contempt that resides in your heart. Will you trust His plan to the point of forgiveness? Deliverance *is* available. Healing *is* here. Don't stop short of blossoming into the freest version of you. The Father has wrapped your identity in His identity. The past has no bearing on your future… unless you refuse to release. Will you trust your Father enough to forgive your father?

[14] Deliver me from the guilt of bloodshed, O God, the God of my salvation, and my tongue shall sing aloud of Your righteousness. [15] O Lord, open my lips, And my mouth shall show forth Your praise. Psalm 51:14-15

Maybe you're thinking, "Mine is the only blood that has been shed. I am the one who has been battered, bruised, and misused." Most sincerely I must say to you, murder begins in the heart. You may have never caused your father physical harm, but is it possible that you have unknowingly assaulted him time and time again? Be honest. Have your words slain him?

[21]"You have heard that our ancestors were told, 'You must not murder. If you commit murder, you are subject to judgment.' [22] But I say, if you are even angry with someone, you are subject to judgment! If you call someone an idiot, you are in danger of being brought before the court. And if you curse someone, you are in danger of the fires of hell. Matthew 5:21-22, NLT

[8] But no man can tame the tongue. It is an unruly evil, full of deadly poison. [9] With it we bless our God and Father, and with it we curse men, who have been made in the similitude of God. [10] Out of the same mouth proceed blessing and cursing. My brethren, these things ought not to be so. [11] Does a spring send forth fresh water and bitter from the same opening? [12] Can a fig tree, my brethren, bear olives, or a grapevine bear figs? Thus no spring yields both salt water and fresh. James 3:8-12

Truth is sometimes a hard pill to swallow. Harboring unresolved strife and contempt positions us for judgment. Ouch! Wait. It gets better. God loves you far too much to leave you as you are. It is with lovingkindness that He draws you to Himself. (See Jeremiah 31:3). Cleansing happens in close proximity. It is His will that no darkened crevice or buried hurt go unnoticed. He wants to purify you. His Word revolutionizes your thinking so that bitter and sweet water no longer attempt to simultaneously flow from the fountain of your mouth. Your lips were made for praising. Your heart was made to give and receive love. It has been shattered. God knows you are broken, but His hope is to heal you. Now is the time. Forgiveness is an integral part of the process.

It is time to *truly* let go and let God. Let God be God. Unclench your fists; withdraw your nails from the anger that you're gripping. Your feelings are warranted. You were wronged. God understands that more than anyone. However, these feelings you're harboring aren't helping you. They are killing you slowly. Release. It's time for you to heal.

[16] *For You do not desire sacrifice, or else I would give it; You do not delight in burnt offering.* [17] *The sacrifices of God are a broken spirit, a broken and a contrite heart— these, O God, You will not despise.* Psalm 51:16-17

You are to be that David-like sacrifice – broken, repentant, and transparent. Be honest with God. Pour out your heart. You are tired of fighting a losing battle. No longer content with donning a victim status, you are ready to claim your victory. Fear urges you to cower in a place of familiarity. Don't do it! Anger is what you know. It's time to know something different. Faith says, "Move forward. Greater days are yet to come." God has more for you, but His riches cannot be received until you empty yourself of ill feelings toward your father and everyone else that you have been holding hostage in the confines of your mind. Some have apologized, far more have not. Admission of guilt isn't the basis by which you decide to forgive. No ma'am! Whether someone acknowledges their wrong or not, whether "I'm sorry" crosses their lips or not, you still have the responsibility to forgive. Simply put: forgive and you shall be forgiven.

[14] *"For if you forgive men their trespasses, your heavenly Father will also forgive you.* [15] *But if you do not forgive men their trespasses, neither will your Father forgive your trespasses.* Matthew 6:14-15

It is human nature to magnify the flaws of others while minimizing ours. As much as we hate to admit it, this is a matter of pride. You want and need God's forgiveness, but it is a struggle to forgive those who have hurt you. God knows. And because it is such a challenge, He isn't calling you to do it in your strength. Trust the Holy Spirit to be your guide and source of power. He will forever lead you in the way of love, peace, and true holiness. Your heart may not soften overnight. More than likely, it won't. Forgiveness is not a feeling; it is an intentional act of obedience. Be still and know that He is God. Never will the Lord require something of you without equipping you for the task. Trust Him to lead you down the path of forgiveness. Release is therapy, boo!

[12] Therefore, as the elect of God, holy and beloved, put on tender mercies, kindness, humility, meekness, longsuffering; [13] bearing with one another, and forgiving one another, if anyone has a complaint against another; even as Christ forgave you, so you also must do. [14] But above all these things put on love, which is the bond of perfection. [15] And let the peace of God rule in your hearts, to which also you were called in one body; and be thankful. Colossians 3:12-15

Father,

Search the heart of Your daughter and know her ways. Listen to her words and know her thoughts. Hear the pain behind the laughter. Know the brokenness behind the smile. As desperately as she wants to move forward in You, the turmoil of her past attempts to prevent her feet from walking in peace. That is not Your will. Your Word says *when the enemy comes in like a flood, Your Spirit will lift up a standard against him.* (Isaiah 59:19). He has flooded her mind with negativity for too long; I thank You that Your standard is being lifted. I thank You for the healing that is taking place right now. Lord, I praise You for being mighty to save. You are well able to deliver us from our own life-stealing thoughts. In the name of Jesus, I call the chains of hate, anger, resentment, and revenge loosed right now! Whom the Son sets free is free indeed! Your daughter is free to dance in Your presence. She is free to sing Your praises. She is free to receive Your forgiveness because holy boldness has risen up in her spirit. She has found the strength needed to forgive others. Your daughter is free in Jesus' name! Amen. So be it!

Release Therapy: Thoughts of Revival

Here is your place to purge. Write your thoughts – good and bad – associated with forgiving all who have wronged you.

Depths of Forgiveness

Jazzmin

Surrender came age nineteen. I gave my life to Christ alone in my dorm room. After what felt like hours of crying happy tears in His presence, I got up and looked at myself in the mirror. A wide smile stretched across my tear-streaked face.

Wow! So, THIS is what I look like?

Freedom was beautiful and peaceful and affirming. For the first time ever, I could see me. I saw Jazzmin! That day I began to think and walk differently. Revelation hit me. Everything previously experienced was meant to happen because it led me to the Lord. The price was worth it! The path prepared my heart to receive His Spirit. Even my pain had a hand in leading me into the Father's arms.

A man's heart plans his way, but the Lord directs his steps. Proverbs 16:9

Thank the Lord for ordered steps. My new found freedom was a bit shaken when I soon came to realize that redemption has an element of sacrifice mixed in. *You must honor your father and mother.* The Lord spoke matter-of-factly to me one day during prayer. In that moment He began to show me the pain endured by my parents. He allowed me to see them through a lens of compassion and understanding. This was so new to me. Truthfully, extending grace to my mother wasn't too hard. She raised me. The situation with my father was a different matter.

I have always known my dad. Actually, it may be more accurate to say I have always known *of* him. He was in and out of my life – here for a while, gone for a while. As time progressed, it seemed as though money was his love language… or maybe a way to make his absence more tolerable. He would pick up my brother and me for a shopping trip and dinner. And just like that he would disappear again. The last vanishing act lasted from fifth grade until eight grade. He reappeared in an attempt to salvage the lost years. The relationship between my dad and I was on the mends but my heart wasn't. Releasing the past was so hard! He left me for years with no explanation and now, all these years later, God was requiring me (me!) to forgive *him*. To say was a process is an understatement.

If you don't forgive your daddy the unforgiveness will carry over into your marriage. You will expect your husband to be everything your father wasn't, and that is not his place.

Over and over again, I heard the same warning. My boyfriend and I began dating a year after I received salvation; he proposed when I was twenty-one. By this time, my dad and I had an okay relationship. It wasn't what I wanted it to be, but progress had been made. My husband-to-be deserved a healed wife. Beyond that, the Father couldn't forgive me if I continued to not forgive my father. Matthew 6:15, TLB reads, "Your heavenly Father will forgive you if you forgive those who sin against you; but if you refuse to forgive them, He will not forgive you." Forgiveness wasn't optional; it was a must!

I want you to give me away at my wedding. I want you included in this moment but you're going to have to show me that you care. I want you to get to know my fiancé and spend time with us. That's how I'll know you will be here.

Maybe that sounds ultimatum-ish but my expectations needed to be clear. Disappearing and reappearing were no longer options. It was more than a wedding, more than one day with perfect pictures. He was my father, the man who would eventually be a grandfather to my children. My grown woman heart still yearned for a consistent daddy. To my surprise, he came through! He honored my request for quality time with my fiancé and me. He walked me down the aisle when the big day came. He even paid for the wedding! Most importantly, we were able to have real conversations about the past and discuss plans about moving forward. This seems like a fitting place for "The End" but it's not.

I found myself in a better relationship with my father but still scarred by the past. Where was healing? How was I supposed to get to a place of wholeness??? The pain kept popping up with every new stage of life. The whirlwind of negative emotions seemed to be intensified by marriage. Prior to marriage, I had never experienced living so closely with a man. I had no previous knowledge of spiritual headship, and this idea of submission wasn't working for me! I was trying to figure out how to navigate this new season God's way. The more I prayed for the Lord to help me, the worse I became. Lashing out at my husband, having a bad attitude, and poppin' off for the smallest things – I was a wreck! I couldn't figure out why it was so hard for me to receive my husband's wise counsel. I didn't know why trusting him was a struggle. Never once did my husband try to use his position against me. Still, in heated moments I would find myself saying, "You ain't my daddy!" That's it! I said it even though I couldn't see it. My feelings couldn't differentiate between my husband and my father. My heart was more hardened than healed. I was doing exactly what I attempted to avoid.

Although I tried not to, I was punishing my husband for things he had never done. He was bearing the burden of my broken heart. Reading *Daddy, Unbreak My Heart* caused light to shine on the dark places of my heart. I love my husband more than anyone else on earth, yet my hateful actions conveyed a contradicting message. The problem was in trying to connect forgiving my dad with him meeting surface-level requirements. Taking an honest look back, I now see I tried to make him perform for forgiveness. What I failed to do was acknowledge the anger and bitterness that had taken root deep within my heart.

[23] Search me, O God, and know my heart; try me, and know my anxieties; [24] and see if there is any wicked way in me, and lead me in the way everlasting. Psalm 139:23-24

Christ is the vine; I am the branch. Apart from Him, I can bear no good fruit. (See John 15:1-4). As I abide in Him, He carefully and mercifully walks me through the uprooting of the negativity afflicting my heart. I have cried and screamed and journaled through the process. I have admitted hard truths and spoken much needed apologies. The past doesn't get to define me. Bitterness doesn't get to overtake me. I am who God says I am! My father wasn't always present; however, my Father never stopped watching over me. The more I come to know the depth, width, and height of His love, the more clearly I see myself as a reflection of His image. The Father never held me hostage to my imperfections; neither will I hold my father hostage for his. All is forgiven. I can clearly see the new me. Free from the weight of unforgiveness, I see me.

About Jazzmin

Jazzmin is a young lady after God's own heart! She serves the Lord by serving others. Currently, Jazzmin attends Lipscomb University on a full academic scholarship. As a Social Work major, she hopes to one day impact the lives of youth through prevention, intervention, and policy reform. Jazzmin actively engages her community through independent mentorship and Apartment Life, a non-profit organization that she and her husband serve through planned activities and community partnerships.

CHAPTER SEVEN

Double-Break

Generational Patterns

And the LORD said to [Rebekah]: "Two nations are in your womb, two peoples shall be separated from your body; one people shall be stronger than the other, and the older shall serve the younger." Genesis 25:23

One womb with two nations, ordained to be divided. What mother wants to hear that?!?! Rebekah waited so long for motherhood; however, there was no forewarning of this major detail. She had no inkling that she was destined to conceive a dueling duo. Could it be that her answered prayer was the continuation of a generational problem?

Before conception, Rebekah's husband, Isaac, pleaded with the Lord on her behalf. (See Genesis 25:21). He believed in the power of God and refused to accept infertility as the final say-so of his lineage. Having passed through the womb of a once barren woman, it's likely that Isaac grew up hearing about God's favor at work in the lives of his parents, Abraham and Sarah. Isaac was not only a miracle baby but also the seed of promise. He was the one through whom God's promise to Abraham would flow. Like his father, Isaac put his faith to work. Also like his faith, division came to his household.

27 So the boys grew. And Esau was a skillful hunter, a man of the field; but Jacob was a mild man, dwelling in tents. 28 And Isaac loved Esau because he ate of his game, but Rebekah loved Jacob. Genesis 25:27-28

We draw nearer to those to whom we relate. However, there is a reason why James 2:9 warns against the sin of partiality. Often, favoritism and rejection are two sides of the same coin. When favoritism has its way hearts become brittle and broken. As the root of rejection stretches out, manipulation and desperation are granted space to roam freely. Esau was a reflection of his father; Jacob was more like his mother. The differences shown by their parents made these brothers further contenders.

5 Now Rebekah was listening when Isaac spoke to Esau his son. And Esau went to the field to hunt game and to bring it. 6 So Rebekah spoke to Jacob her son, saying, "Indeed I heard your father speak to Esau your brother, saying, 7 'Bring me game and make savory food for me, that I may eat it and bless you in the presence of the Lord before my death.' [8] Now therefore, my son, obey my voice according to what I command you. [9] Go now to the flock and bring me from there two choice kids of the goats, and I will make savory food from them for your father, such as he loves. [10] Then you shall take it to your father that he may eat it, and that he may bless you before his death." Genesis 27:5-10

Oooh, messy mama! By this point, Jacob had already tricked Esau out of his birthright. Now, he was conspiring with his mother to take his brother's blessing as well. It was the word of the Lord that the younger brother would serve the older, but surely God's Word could be accomplished without deception. When the Word goes forth, it does not return void; it performs the very thing it is sent to do. (See Isaiah 55:11). Attempting to do a God-thing in a human way is a recipe for disaster. Maybe Rebekah's bloodline was marred by tricksters and Jacob had too much of her in him. Or maybe Jacob was the spitting image of his grandfather – knowledgeable of the promise but bothered by the timing.

You see, whether it is acknowledged or not, an unaddressed past can show up in our present. Your father hurt you. Who hurt your father? Your father rejected you. Who pushed him down the path of rejection? This isn't about making excuses for him; it's about gaining an understanding of what came before him. The cycles we identify are the cycles we can break. Being born into a generational trend or curse does not leave you powerless to change the trajectory of your lineage. Hun, you are a change agent! Lean in and learn from the past.

³ Then Sarai, Abram's wife, took Hagar her maid, the Egyptian, and gave her to her husband Abram to be his wife, after Abram had dwelt ten years in the land of Canaan. ⁴ So he went in to Hagar, and she conceived. And when she saw that she had conceived, her mistress became despised in her eyes. Genesis 16:3-4

According to Pastor Dharius Daniels, it is possible to hear right and interpret wrong. That's because revelation has layers. Our humanness makes it tempting to receive a word and run with the word without giving it time to mature in our hearts. God's promise to Abram was that an heir would come from his body and his descendants would outnumber the stars. (See Genesis 15:4-5). Abram heard the promise but didn't allow time for it to unfold.

¹¹ And the Angel of the Lord said to [Hagar]: "Behold, you are with child, and you shall bear a son. You shall call his name Ishmael, because the Lord has heard your affliction. ¹² He shall be a wild man; his hand shall be against every man, and every man's hand against him. And he shall dwell in the presence of all his brethren." Genesis 16:11-12

Again, attempting to do a God-thing in a human way is a recipe for disaster. The next layer of revelation to come was that Sarah would be the mother of Abraham's promised heir. The work of patience is to make us perfect and complete, lacking nothing. (See James 1:4). Impatience creates problems that contend with God's perfect promise and war against our identity.

[19] Then God said: "No, Sarah your wife shall bear you a son, and you shall call his name Isaac; I will establish My covenant with him for an everlasting covenant, and with his descendants after him. [20] And as for Ishmael, I have heard you. Behold, I have blessed him, and will make him fruitful, and will multiply him exceedingly. He shall beget twelve princes, and I will make him a great nation. [21] But My covenant I will establish with Isaac, whom Sarah shall bear to you at this set time next year." Genesis 17:19-21

Two wombs. Two nations. One father. Multi-generational impact. Abraham received a promise but inserted Sarah's solution, thus resulting in the necessary separation of Ishmael from Isaac. Isaac fathered Esau and Jacob, and a wedge was driven between the two. In the next generation, Joseph – born to yet another barren mother – was sold into slavery by his older brothers. Do you see what I see? Here we have four generations of contentious cycles and problematic patterns. Could it be that there is more to what you feel than what you see? Is it possible that the root of your pain originated from the fruit of preceding generations?

The fact of the matter is fathers are humans, and humans are flawed. This fact does not negate your feelings. Your hurt is real and worth acknowledging. Also to be recognized is the past before your past. Generational cycles, patterns, and curses can produce perpetual heartbreak. Just as dysfunction creates breaking, breaking destroys dysfunction.

⁴⁵ And so it is written, "The first man Adam became a living being." The last Adam became a life-giving spirit. 46 However, the spiritual is not first, but the natural, and afterward the spiritual. ⁴⁷ The first man was of the earth, made of dust; the second Man is the Lord from heaven.

I Corinthians 15:45-47

The last Adam, who is Christ, came to rectify the first Adam's wrongs. Divinity came to demolish dysfunction. The Spirt accomplished what flesh could not. Our heavenly Father chose not to play favorites. Instead, He sent His only begotten Son to earth for the redemption and healing of all His children. The veil has been torn; separation from the Father is no more. The sting of the father's sin is no match for the Father's love. Reconciliation, righteousness, and a revived heart are the inheritance of the King's daughters.

Raise your head and wipe your eyes. The dysfunction you lived through has no right to define you. You are a daughter of the Most High. The curses and patterns plaguing you thus far have no authority over your future. The brokenness is breaking. Healing is here. Receive it.

Therefore, if anyone is in Christ, he is a new creation; old things have passed away; behold, all things have become new. II Corinthians 5:17

Father God,

I thank You for the second breaking. In the name of Jesus, the brokenness that once calloused Your daughter's heart is lifting. Soften and heal her heart, Lord. Give her eyes to see that nothing about her identity warranted mistreatment. The patterns of her past (and beyond) have no power over her present and future. Sweep through her spirit with Your Spirit. Be her very present help in this time of need. Father, we thank You for healing in the breaking. Amen.

Double-Break: Thoughts of Revival

What generational cycles, patterns, or curses need to broke off of your life? List them, and write a prayer to declare their breaking.

Wounded

Dolores

My earthly father was 16 when I was born. At 8 pounds and 10 ounces, I was the first of many unwanted pregnancies. My father lived on the inner city streets of Dallas. Did he have a home? Yes, but the night lights and accessible drugs called him to a life of violence and abuse, creating an ongoing cycle.

Hey, Mija! How are you doing?

I remember my tiny, dirty feet walking down the cold hallway of Lusterics Correctional Facility. Unlike in the movies where you could see your loved one through a big clear glass, we were in a small cubicle with a little black reflective glass. It served the purpose of reminding offenders that they were separated from the world. Even the human decency of seeing his 3-year-old daughter wasn't an option for my dad. I held on to that beige-colored phone wanting so badly for him to say, "I'm coming home."

I was too young to understand the crime he committed. All I knew was that my protector and friend was so far away, and the only way I could connect with him was through the hollow sound of his voice echoing down that cold, gray hall.

Several years passed before I saw my father again. To provide a glimpse of the humanity in his world, we journeyed hand-in-hand on a bus ride I'll never forget. We drove past tall buildings and clean playgrounds while venturing deep into the inner city. "Never forget the people who have no place to go." Those were the words he spoke while handing me a tray and motioning for me to join the food line at a homeless shelter. Were we homeless? No. We were here because his self-worth told him he deserved nothing better. After this experience, my little heart searched for my dad on every street corner and under every bypass. Drugs called him to the streets; we had no way of knowing when we would see him.

I was fourteen the last time I saw my dad. Going in and out of prison was normal by this point. Heroin had control of his mind, and he was convinced we were his enemies. He believed *I* was his enemy! The wildness in his eyes was proof that he had no comprehension of me being his daughter. I watched as he was placed in the back of a police car. The charge: child abuse.

Having a father figure-type relationship is not something that gives me comfort. Nineteen years ago, I received Christ as my Savior. His Father became my heavenly Father. On rare occasions, the Father reveals to me His kindness, goodness, and selflessness through father figures within the church. All these years later, I deflect the simplest of male interaction.

It's a wonder that I was able to marry a strong, godly man despite the many men that came along. Through my husband and the birth of our daughter, God has painted deep, vibrant colors over old memories. My husband's love for our daughter reveals the love of a gentle giant, my Creator Father. I see the Father in their laughter-filled moments and when they sing songs of praise in unison. Outside of this up close and personal experience, I may have never known God's ability to use children as a mechanism for healing adult hurts.

My relationship with God remains on the baby steps. More descriptively, it's like a man patiently waiting to catch a fish – I'm the fish! I wish I were further along in my 20-year walk with the Lord. The other day I compared living for God to a spider's web. The lines are so thin and easily missed. I questioned how I could live this out. My husband – in all his wisdom – said, "God is the sticky." God gives us the ability to stay connected to Him. He provides the stickiness.

My earthly father was a distant memory until recently. My sister, who is not saved, asked if I think I should visit him. Without a thought, my answer was, "No." It was then that I knew this was still an issue. How could I show my sister the love of the Father while simultaneously revealing the unforgiveness being harbored in my heart towards our father? This caught my attention. God was putting a spotlight on that wound. I believe God is flipping through my book and letting me know it's time to start writing on the pages concerning my earthly father; hence, this testimony.

God is so gentle. He knows when your heart is ready to begin the healing process. His timing perfectly aligns with our willingness to work through the wounds. My earthly father is imprisoned and in poor health. He's up for parole in 2025. Hopefully, his newfound faith in Judaism will cut the tie to violence and chaos. He still doesn't know Jesus, but as long as there is breath in his lungs, there is a chance for him to receive salvation.

About Dolores

Dolores lives in Murfreesboro, Tennessee with her husband, Nick, and their children. She is the founder and publisher of Rutherford County's *Life Line Magazine*, a publication aimed toward promoting a Christian perspective on the topic of mental health. For more about *Life Line*, please visit

www.rc-lifelinemagazine.com

CHAPTER EIGHT

Positioned

& Relieved

Abiding in His Presence

¹He who dwells in the secret place of the Most High Shall abide under the shadow of the Almighty. ² I will say of the Lord, "He is my refuge and my fortress; My God, in Him I will trust." ⁴ He shall cover you with His feathers, and under His wings you shall take refuge; His truth shall be your shield and buckler. Psalm 91:1-2, 4

To *abide* means to stay, reside or dwell; to continue in a particular condition, attitude, or relationship. When you abide in the secret place of the Most High, you are positioned for comfort and protection. Boo, you no longer need to protect you! As the Spirit of the Lord was with the children of Israel, so He is with you. He goes before you to lead the way into your future.

21 And the Lord went before them by day in a pillar of cloud to lead the way, and by night in a pillar of fire to give them light, so as to go by day and night. 22 He did not take away the pillar of cloud by day or the pillar of fire by night from before the people. Exodus 13:21-22

He stands behind you to prevent the oppression of your past from overtaking your present.

19 And the Angel of God, who went before the camp of Israel, moved and went behind them; and the pillar of cloud went from before them and stood behind them. 20 So it came between the camp of the Egyptians and the camp of Israel. Thus it was a cloud and darkness to the one, and it gave light by night to the other, so that the one did not come near the other all that night. Exodus 14:19-20

Even as you walk through wilderness seasons, He is with you. He is your refuge and fortress, your peace and your joy. You have been relieved from the pressure of being your own protection. Calm down. Breathe. Now, abide in His presence.

You will show me the path of life; In Your presence is fullness of joy; At Your right hand are pleasures forevermore. Psalm 16:11

He goes before you, He comes behind you, and all the while His Spirit is with you. Let Jesus' words ring true: *I am the vine, you are the branches. He who abides in Me, and I in him, bears much fruit; for without Me you can do nothing.* (John 15:5). Everything you were ever meant to be is encompassed in your Christ-identity. It is He who shows you the path of life. In His presence there is fullness of joy and pleasures that could never be attained through natural measures. Abide in Him. You were meant to thrive. Your life is destined to bear much fruit, good fruit. Abide.

With His presence comes strength. It is written, *the joy of the Lord is your strength.* (Nehemiah 8:10). You have tried carrying your burdens but the weight was too much, right? Because you are incapable of healing your pain, you tried to bury it. Still, the wounds run deep and no amount of depth has been able to keep your hurt concealed. The key to your recovery is to dwell in the shadows of His wings. You aren't hiding and you aren't weak or cowardly. You are resting – something life's circumstances haven't afforded you much of an opportunity to do.

⁴ One thing I have desired of the Lord, that will I seek: that I may dwell in the house of the Lord all the days of my life, to behold the beauty of the Lord, and to inquire in His temple. ⁵ For in the time of trouble He shall hide me in His pavilion; in the secret place of His tabernacle He shall hide me; He shall set me high upon a rock. Psalm 27:4-5

Every house isn't a home. Though inhabited, every dwelling place does not exude peace and safety. But in the house of the Lord, you can rest. Ahh. Breathe, boo. Because you are His temple, no searching is required. Where you are, He is. And where He is, there is freedom. (See II Corinthians 3:17). Your past can't bind you. Disappointments cannot suppress you. You are an overcomer! Reject every self-deprecating lie you have dared to believe, because you are loved and approved by your heavenly Father.

When my father and my mother forsake me, then the Lord will take care of me. Psalm 27:10

Humans are humans and humans are flawed. They won't always live up the standards of their roles. God is not to be grouped with those who disappoint. He will never fail you. He will never leave you. Never means never. *I will not leave you comfortless: I will come to you* (John 14:18, KJV). The New King James Version exchanges orphans for comfortless. *I will not leave you orphans.* God will not leave you parentless. It is not His will for you to exist without parental covering, guidance, and provision. Above all, He is your source. He is your all-in-all.

When others walk away, God is there. When fathers and mothers are unable or unwilling to do their part in the lives of their children, the Lord is there. You have always held a special place in His heart, even when you weren't aware of the overflowing love He has for you. He is here for you – always has been.

See beyond what is seen. Facts are a matter of perception. They are "truths" based on observation. For years upon years the enemy has marred your view and distorted your thinking in an attempt to lure you into believing that God is your adversary. The fact is your dad wasn't there as he should have been. His absence damaged you. You experienced brokenness as a result. There are those of you whose father's presence rather than his absence was the problem. Instead of loving and protecting, he abused, misused, and attempted to destroy you. You, too, are broken. Factually speaking, you know other women who carry their hurt like a badge of honor. They shut others out for fear of being hurt or shunned once again. The fact remains that some never receive their healing. That's not you! Your reality as a child of God moves beyond the facts. Healing is here.

¹ Oh, give thanks to the Lord, for He is good! For His mercy endures forever. ² Let the redeemed of the Lord say so, whom He has redeemed from the hand of the enemy. Psalm 107:1-2

You are free! You are positioned in righteousness and relieved from the constraints of your past. My dear, you are not broken beyond repair. Jesus came to offer *beauty for your ashes, oil of joy for your mourning, and a garment of praise for your spirit of heaviness.* (See Isaiah 61:3). Abide in His presence.

Lord God in heaven,

I thank You that as Your Word goes forth, the scales are being knocked from this precious one's eyes. As she begins to see You more and more for Who You are, she is realizing that Your hand of grace and protection has been there. As rough as life has been, she is still standing. It is by Your grace. Although her heart was hardened, Your love remained persistent. Thank You for loving her so patiently. Continue to have Your way. Reveal Your promises and heal by Your Spirit. Uncover Satan's lies and cover her in Your truth. May she dwell in Your presence forever. Amen.

Why is healing a priority now?

In Line for Healing

Ruth

My father was not a mean man. He was a hardworking, Christian man who instilled a love for God in me. Our family was more reliable than the post office when it came to church attendance. Neither snow, nor rain nor gloom of night would keep us from the house of the Lord on Sundays. I was not physically or verbally abused. My dad was always present in my life. By now you must be wondering what my issue with my father could possibly be. He withdrew his attention from me, that's how. While that may not seem like a big deal, it is when you are eight years old and your love language is quality time.

My sister's autism diagnosis was the beginning of the end. My fantastic relationship with my earthly daddy was over and it never recovered. My father shifted his attention from me, the "okay one" as he put it, to the one whom he believed needed him more.

Even if my father and mother abandon me, the Lord with hold me close. Psalm 27:10

It took almost ten years of therapy to start valuing myself enough to stop falling for the wrong men and giving myself away. Breaking the cycle was a struggle, because those men gave me the attention I so desperately craved. I made the choice to forgive but healing was slow in coming. A few months before my father passed away from a sudden illness, I shared with him that I although I loved him as my father, I did not like him very much. His response was, "I don't know what I did but maybe it was something I didn't do that made you feel this way." At that time, I still wasn't able to verbalize exactly what happened to make me feel the way I did about him.

I shed no tears when my father passed away. My sadness was reserved for the hurt and loss experienced by my mother and sister. My mother had lost a companion and my sister lost her dad. I, on the other hand, was glad that I no longer had to deal with him.

Fast forward to 2017. By this time, I am eight years into marriage with a wonderful man who has walked with me during many years of therapy. He has been the salve on the self-inflicted wounds of my youth. He was the only man that didn't run from the messy parts of my life. Still, more was needed. God knew just how to initiate healing.

I was waiting in line for one of the general sessions at Christy Wright's *Business Boutique*. A burst of boldness prompted me to step out of my comfort zone and speak to the woman behind me. She happened to be an aspiring author and speaker. I asked her what she'd written and she began telling me about *Daddy, Unbreak My Heart*. As we talked, I realized I was still hurting, still angry that my father took my portion of his affection and gave a double portion to my sister. Speaking with LaToya for just ten minutes had me teary-eyed. I still had wounds. Next thing you know, she whipped out a copy of her book and gifted it to me! I was so excited to get started on it in an attempt to get more relief.

I pulled out my bible and started reading the book and studying the scripture referenced throughout each chapter. The words fell flat. You see, I have heard all these words since I was in the womb. I was expecting something fresh and new and it wasn't. I had heard it all before. Rather than just set the book aside, I asked the Lord to enable me to see His Word with fresh eyes. My heart needed a fresh stirring. The bitterness I held towards my father had hardened my heart. Yes, I had forgiven the man who was the source of my pain, the pain that influenced so many of the destructive decisions during my youth. But my heart was calloused. The years of self-inflicted abuse had created a tough skin that only God's Word could slough away.

And we know that God causes all things to work together for the good of those who love God and are called according to his purpose for them. Romans 8:28

    The Lord answered my prayer. I started the book from the beginning, and this time the pages came alive! I was finally seeing what He always wanted me to see. Although my earthly father was greatly flawed, my Heavenly Daddy was perfect and loved me with His perfect love. *Unbreak* helped me to see that of all the things my earthly father did wrong, the one thing he did right was to introduce me to my Heavenly Father, in whom there is no error.

    The healing that started in November 2017 continues. Because my eyes have been opened to the realization of Whose I am, the Lord has given me a deeper understanding into my past. I see how pain grows roots, and those roots bear self-destructive fruit. *Unbreak* led to the uprooting of bitterness in my life. I can move forward with a lighter heart.

    The most recent wave of healing came at the start of 2019 when I finally took responsibility for the harmful decisions I made when I was young. You see, while my choices were influenced by my pain, it doesn't change the fact that they were *my* decisions. My Heavenly Father had been with me through all of it, and I would have avoided a lot of unnecessary pain had I just sought Him the way I'd been taught as a child.

I don't know if all my healing will come this side of heaven, but I know there is more to come and I trust my Heavenly Father to bring it. I am grateful for the grace He has shown me through it all.

My old self has been crucified with Christ. It is no longer I who live but Christ lives in me. So I live in this earthly body by trusting the Son of God. Galatians 2:20

About Ruth

Ruth is the daughter of Cuban immigrants, wife to a wonderful man, and momma to four crazy fur-children. More than anything, she is a lover of Jesus. Now in her 40's, Ruth is learning what it means to be a daughter of the King. She and her family are currently embarking on a Spirit-led, cross-country journey of fearlessness and freedom. Follow their adventures at https://thegerkyjourney.wixsite.com.

CHAPTER NINE

Casting Your Cares

Mind Shift

Casting your cares upon Him, for He cares for you. I Peter 5:7

When you feel cast away, cast your cares upon the Lord. When you find yourself tormented by hurtful memories, find rest in the presence of God. Relinquish your cares to Him. That sounds great but I imagine you're wondering how.

[29] Take My yoke upon you and learn from Me, for I am gentle and lowly in heart, and you will find rest for your souls. [30] For My yoke is easy and My burden is light. Matthew 11:29-30

This concept may be foreign, so allow me to explain. A yoke is a wooden beam that connects two animals and attaches them to a plow. This equips them to work as a team to accomplish a task too burdensome for one to bear.

Ahhhh! Yep, now you're getting it! Jesus is saying, "Link up with Me!" Instead of being overwhelmed and overloaded, His offer is a yoke that produces freedom. He desires to partner with you on this healing journey. Together, you two will plow through the pain of your past. Hun, problems have to be uncovered in order for you to recover. Rejection's root has to be pulled up. The fallow ground of your heart HAS to be tilled. Healing cannot flow from an uncultivated soul.

Loosen your grip. Trade your bondage and burdens for freedom in the Spirit. There is no burden that Christ isn't willing to bust through on your behalf. Trust Him. Release your broken pieces to Him. Give Him your concerns. Find rest for your soul as the Comforter teaches you to think, speak, and live according to God's will. Freedom is yours. Do you want it? Are you willing to join forces with your Help?

3 For though we walk in the flesh, we do not war according to the flesh. 4 For the weapons of our warfare are not carnal but mighty in God for pulling down strongholds, 5 casting down arguments and every high thing that exalts itself against the knowledge of God, bringing every thought into captivity to the obedience of Christ. II Corinthians 10:3-5

War is waging and its battlefield is your mind. Back and forth, you find yourself constantly struggling between dueling realities: faith and fear, holy boldness and cowardice, strength and weakness, blessed assurance and oppressive doubt. As desperately as you want to see yourself through the eyes of your Father, your father's influence has skewed your perception. Dear God, give Your daughter eyes to see and ears to hear as You alleviate her heart of its burdens.

See the spirit behind the situation. *For we do not wrestle against flesh and blood, but against principalities, against powers, against the rulers of the darkness of this age, against spiritual hosts of wickedness in the heavenly places.* (Ephesians 6:12). Though this may be difficult to grasp, your father is not your enemy. He was a *tool* of the enemy. He was used, and you were hurt. See beyond the surface. Spiritual battles cannot be won by natural methods. Your victory will not come by fighting flesh with flesh. Allowing bitterness, rage, and any other negative emotions to fester in your heart will lead to your spiritual demise.

Walk in the light. Walk in the revelation of Whose you are. You are God's daughter. Though principalities, powers, and rulers of darkness have come against you, the Holy Spirit of God Almighty exists within you. You are of God. That guarantees that you are an overcomer, because *greater is He that is in you than he that is in the world.* (I John 4:4).

You are empowered to succeed. Clothe yourself in the full armor of God and stand. Stand? Yes, *take up the whole armor of God, that you may be able to withstand in the evil day, and having done all, to stand.* (Ephesians 6:13). Prepare for war but cast your cares upon the Lord. It is He who fights your battles.

[14] Stand therefore, having girded your waist with truth, having put on the breastplate of righteousness, [15] and having shod your feet with the preparation of the gospel of peace; [16] above all, taking the shield of faith with which you will be able to quench all the fiery darts of the wicked one. [17] And take the helmet of salvation, and the sword of the Spirit, which is the word of God. Ephesians 6:14-17

To be different, you must first begin to think differently. Bondage begins in your mind. True, you have been a victim, but you will not continue to be oppressed by a victim's mindset. It's time to do away with wrong thinking. Now is the time to root out every lie that has been ascribed to your identity and self-worth. Mind renewal. Mental liberation. Forgiveness. (Yes, I said the f-word...) It's time.

[8] But now is the time to get rid of anger, rage, malicious

behavior, slander, and dirty language. ⁹ Don't lie to each other, for you have stripped off your old sinful nature and all its wicked deeds. ¹⁰ Put on your new nature, and be renewed as you learn to know your Creator and become like him. Colossians 3:8-10, NLT

You are a new woman in Christ. (See II Corinthians 5:17). Walk in that newness. Wrong thinking comes as Satan's attempt to cause you to stumble. A mental makeover is the key to not breaking stride. You see, although your heart has been made new and you have been given the mind of Christ, it is pertinent that you renew your original mind daily. How so? Continually expose it to the Word of God and bring your thought-life captive to the obedience of Christ. Again, to *be* different you must begin to *think* differently.

Whatever things are true, whatever things are noble, whatever things are just, whatever things are pure, whatever things are lovely, whatever things are of good report, if there is any virtue and if there is anything praiseworthy—meditate on these things. Philippians 4:8

God never requires you to do anything that He doesn't enable you to do.

26 I will give you a new heart and put a new spirit within you; I will take the heart of stone out of your flesh and give you a heart of flesh. 27 I will put My Spirit within you and cause you to walk in My statutes, and you will keep My judgments and do them. Ezekiel 36:26-27

For His name's sake – as a testament to the faithful consistency of His character – He has given you a fresh start. Stop looking back and look ahead. The past is concrete but the future is packed with potential. You can continue living from a place of what was or step confidently into the hope and future prepared for you. You choose.

As painful memories and disappointments threaten to replay in your mind, turn them over to God. Acknowledge the Father's grace and mercy toward you, and extend that same grace and mercy to your father. No? You cannot or will not do so? It is written, "But if you do not forgive men their trespasses, neither will your Father forgive your trespasses." (Matthew 6:15). Understand that forgiveness is not the equivalent of ignoring a person's wrongs toward you. To forgive is to acknowledge the pain and still choose to pardon. As long as unforgiveness remains in your heart, you remain yoked to the person who did you dirty. Freedom is in forgiveness. Forgiveness is a choice occurring independent of emotion.

You can replay the bad or choose to think on all things good. Cling to the Word of the Lord. Meditate on His teachings; walk in accordance with His will. The Lord is with you wherever you go, lighting your path and lightening your load. Trust Him. His is the yoke needed in your life. There is nothing that He can't handle. Your baggage could never be too much for Him to bear. Cast your cares on God for He cares so very much for you.

⁸ This Book of the Law shall not depart from your mouth, but you shall meditate in it day and night, that you may observe to do according to all that is written in it. For then you will make your way prosperous, and then you will have good success. ⁹ Have I not commanded you? Be strong and of good courage; do not be afraid, nor be dismayed, for the Lord your God is with you wherever you go. Joshua 1:8-9

Father God,

It is impossible on this side of eternity for us to understand just how far-reaching, life-changing, and pain-healing Your love really is. We seek to know Your love more intimately. As Your child draws near to You, she is comforted in knowing You are drawing near to her as well. Come closer, Lord.

Heal, deliver, and restore. Thank You for the transformation that is taking place in her mind by the power of Your love and grace. Speak to the heart of Your daughter. Help her to clearly discern Your voice and to no longer lean on her own understanding. Walk with her on the path to forgiveness. Give her strength to let go and faith to fully trust You. May an unquenchable hunger and thirst for Your Word rise up in her spirit for the renewing of her mind. You fashioned her according to Your image; right thinking and speaking are Your will.

Purify her mind, O God. Help her to think more like You. Be glorified as her thoughts and words align with Yours. Have Your way in her heart and mind in Jesus' name. Amen.

Casting Your Cares: Thoughts of Revival

Forgiveness is not easy yet it is necessary for your freedom. List the top 3 reasons why you are struggling to forgive. Then, write an honest prayer asking God to help you through these points of struggle.

CHAPTER TEN

Trade Out

Walking in Newness

¹Arise, shine; for your light has come! And the glory of the Lord is risen upon you. ² For behold, the darkness shall cover the earth, and deep darkness the people; but the Lord will arise over you, and His glory will be seen upon you.
Isaiah 60:1-2

YOU ARE NOT WHO YOU USED TO BE. Pause to reflect on the powerful truth of that statement. Darkness has given way to light; old things have been made new. You – yes, you – are free to walk in the revelation of who you are in Christ. Whom the Son sets free is free indeed. Hun, you are free!

¹ "The Spirit of the Lord God is upon Me, because the Lord has appointed Me to preach good tidings to the poor; He has sent Me to heal the brokenhearted, to proclaim liberty to captives, and the openings of the prison to those who are bound; ² to proclaim the acceptable year of the Lord, and the day of vengeance of our God; to comfort all who mourn, ³ to console those who mourn in Zion, to give them beauty for ashes, the oil of joy for mourning, the garment of praise for the spirit of heaviness; that they may be called trees of righteousness, the planting of the Lord, that He may be glorified". Isaiah 61:1-3

Christ made the ultimate trade out on the Cross as He stated, "It is finished." He bowed His head and gave up His Spirit. He came to earth with a mission in His heart and humanity on His mind. Yes, He died so that all could have the opportunity to receive eternal life, but don't think that the scope of His love is so vast that He hasn't taken the time to narrow His focus and zoom in on you. Jesus Christ, fully God and fully man, was appointed to meet with you for such a time as this. He was sent long before you were conceived because God always knew you would need to be freed.

He willingly gave His life for you. Scorned, mocked, and scourged, Christ sacrificed Himself for you to gain the privilege of being considered God's precious one. He did so with no regrets. Yes, He did it for all mankind, but don't hesitate to personalize His valiant act; He did it for *you*. He was anointed to bring you good news, to heal your broken heart, to loose the chains of your captivity, and to clothe you in His righteousness so that you would be in right-standing with the Father, *your* heavenly Father. At this very moment the Holy Spirit is sweeping away the shattered and destitute places of your life; He is dusting away ashes to reveal the hidden beauty of your spirit. The anointing has come to destroy yokes. Dry your eyes and look to the Son. Mourning is over; the heaviness is lifting. Your mouth is being filled with praise from the overflow of joy that has invaded your heart. You are not who you once were; Christ has made you new.

As concrete as the past may be, your future is illuminated with possibilities of greatness. Every second increases the gap between the new you that is alive in Christ and the old you that was bound by circumstances beyond your control. You have been made new. *Where the Spirit of the Lord is, there is liberty* (II Corinthians 3:17). He is in you and you are free.

Continue to fix your eyes on things above. Keep walking in your new nature. Remain persistent in your pursuit of God and knowing Him more. Live! In Jesus's name I urge you to live! For far too long you have lugged around baggage that God never intended for you to bear. Make the trade. Remember, His yoke is easy and His burden is light. The thoughts He thinks about you are good; His plan for you is a life marked by wholeness and victory. By faith receive all that the trade encompasses.

¹ If then you were raised with Christ, seek those things which are above, where Christ is, sitting at the right hand of God.
² Set your mind on things above, not on things on the earth.
³ For you died, and your life is hidden with Christ in God.
Colossians 3:1-3

You are dead, yet you have never been more alive. Allow Paul's words to increase your understanding: *My old self has been crucified with Christ. It is no longer I who live, but Christ lives in me. So I live in this earthly body by trusting in the Son of God, who loved me and gave himself for me* (Galatians 2:20, NLT). That's you. You – that is to say the old you – no longer lives; the Holy Spirit lives *through* you. God is glorified through your submission. He is exalted by your obedience. You live because you accepted the trade that Christ died to make. You, daughter of the Most High God, are free.

Lord,

There aren't enough words available to express our gratitude toward You. Still, we give You thanks and praise for You alone are worthy. This is Your daughter, Your child, one whom You love dearly. Thank You for speaking to her heart, reviving her spirit, and filling her mind with right thoughts. Continue to heal, strengthen, and keep her for Your name's sake. Reveal to her Your plans for her life. Give her purpose and passion. Light her path, O Lord. I pray away any religious or traditional yokes that dare to bind her, for it is Your will that we walk in freedom and relationship with You. Help her to confidently know Your voice. Give her the courage to walk in the victory that You have already provided. Reveal her true worth that can only be known in Your presence. I pray all this in the name of Your Son, Jesus. Amen.

Trade Out: Thoughts of Revival

Whom the Son sets free is free indeed. You, my friend, are free! Reflect on that truth.

CHAPTER ELEVEN

Victim Mentality

vs.

Princess Mentality

Now Presenting a New Normal

38 As Jesus and the disciples continued on their way to Jerusalem they came to a village where a woman named Martha welcomed them into her home. 39 Her sister Mary sat on the floor, listening to Jesus as he talked. 40 But Martha was the jittery type and was worrying over the big dinner she was preparing. Luke 10:38-40, TLB

Tsk tsk, Martha! It is written, "Man shall not live by bread alone, but by every word that proceeds from the mouth of God." (Matthew 4:4). Yet, Martha made more of a fuss over baking bread (or whatever she was cooking) than basking in the presence of the Bread of Life. Let's be real. Although Mary made the wiser decision, we are more inclined to take on the spirit of Martha.

[31] *"Therefore do not worry, saying, 'What shall we eat?' or 'What shall we drink?' or 'What shall we wear?' [32] For after all these things the Gentiles seek. For your heavenly Father knows that you need all these things.* Matthew 6:31-32

Your Father knows your needs, but your father dropped the ball. It is hard to wrap your mind around Divine Dad supplying your every need when deadbeat dad left you with deficits. One is your Shepherd; the other is a shadow of distant memories. One promises to make your cup run over and send goodness and mercy to follow you; the other caused tears to overflow and failed at following up on your wellbeing.

Experience is a good teacher, or so they say. You learned to go here and go there, do this and do that so as not to depend on others. Dependency and disappoint are something like kissing cousins, right? They shouldn't be together, but they are together... and their partnership caused you pain. Set goals and grind. Guard your heart and grow your bank account. It is more soothing to your soul to be in control – to juggle all the balls – rather than stockpiling your confidence in an eternal dad-figure who didn't safeguard you in the first place. Ouch! Too real?

[20] Then Martha, as soon as she heard that Jesus was coming, went and met Him, but Mary was sitting in the

house. 21 Now Martha said to Jesus, "Lord, if You had been here, my brother would not have died. 22 But even now I know that whatever You ask of God, God will give You." 23 Jesus said to her, "Your brother will rise again." 24 Martha said to Him, "I know that he will rise again in the resurrection at the last day." John 11:20-24

Shhh! Do you hear that? That, my friend, is the sound of counterfeit faith.

First of all, You not being here led to my heartbreak. So yeah, Lord, I believe You perform miracles... just not for me. You move mountains and cause walls to fall, but I'll need rock-climbing gear to get over this.

It is possible to know the Word and trust the Word and still disassociate yourself from its wonder-working power. In the beginning was the Word, and the Word was with God, and the Word was God... and the Word became flesh and dwelt among us. (John 1:1,14). In the presence of the Word, Martha accepted defeat. She lacked a revelation of her life wrapped in the Word. Instead of personalizing the power that was in her presence, she settled for being a victim of life's circumstances. Almost.

25 Jesus said to her, "I am the resurrection and the life. He who believes in Me, though he may die, he shall live. 26 And whoever lives and believes in Me shall never die. Do you believe this?" 27 She said to Him, "Yes, Lord, I believe that You are the Christ, the Son of God, who is to come into the world." John 11:25-27

Do you know the Lord? I mean, do you *really* know the Lord? He is the One who reveals to you the path of life. In His presence is fullness of joy and unending pleasures. (See Psalm 16:11). Where His Spirit dwells, freedom abides. (See II Corinthians 3:17). He ALWAYS leads you in triumph! (See II Corinthians 2:14). Your heart has a willingness to believe; logic makes your mind hesitant. Wholeness sounds great, but your life is a whole mess! Hun, what has been does not always have to be. Healing is here. Having the mind of Christ gives you the freedom to think differently. (See I Corinthians 2:16). Identity in Christ gives you the power to live differently.

I have been crucified with Christ: and I myself no longer live, but Christ lives in me. And the real life I now have within this body is a result of my trusting in the Son of God, who loved me and gave himself for me. Galatians 2:20, TLB

The past once defined you. Now, it's time for a new normal.

[38] Then Jesus, again groaning in Himself, came to the tomb. It was a cave, and a stone lay against it. [39] Jesus said, "Take away the stone." Martha, the sister of him who was dead, said to Him, "Lord, by this time there is a stench, for he has been dead four days." [40] Jesus said to her, "Did I not say to you that if you would believe you would see the glory of God?" John 11:38-40

It doesn't matter how long rejection has bound you or the depths of the darkness around you. Faith in Christ can overcome whatever funk you may be in. He is able and willing to move on your behalf. Unworthy, irredeemable, and unlovable – these are all lies from the mouth of the enemy. Christ believed you were worth His crucifixion. You are redeemed by the Blood. You are unconditionally and unequivocally loved by the Father. If you press in by faith, you will see the glory of God rest on your life. If you are willing to loosen the grip on all that hurts you, the Father will heal you.

Friend, you were victimized, but you are not a victim. You are a daughter of the King. The Word wrapped Himself in flesh to wrap you in new life. You are not your past. Lift your head and put on a princess' mentality. Enter into the presence of your Lord.

Dear Heavenly Father,

Words cannot express our gratitude for the privilege of coming before Your throne of grace. Here is Your daughter – hurting, yet hopeful. She is broken but at peace with the pieces. She is now ready to place the pieces in Your hands. Comfort and heal, Lord. Lead her along the path of sweet surrender and surround her with Your love. Teach her the truth about who she is in You – redeemed, restored, and revived.

Victim Mentality vs. Princess Mentality: Thoughts of Revival

Write your personal definition of a princess' mentality.

CHAPTER TWELVE

Listen Up

The Process of Newness

One thing I have desired of the Lord, that will I seek: that I may dwell in the house of the Lord all the days of my life, to behold the beauty of the Lord, and to inquire in His temple.
Psalm 27:4

The Lord is as near as your heart. His desire is for you to continually draw nearer, to dive more deeply into His presence. Is this process of increased intimacy your desire? Allow me to explain before you answer. Intimacy: *into me see*. The Lord knows your heart, but His desire is to reveal the richness of His heart to you. Christ reigns as your Savior; genuine fellowship connects the two of you as friends. Are you ready to encounter the Lord on another level? Draw deeply from the well that never runs dry.

No longer do I call you servants, for a servant does not know what his master is doing; but I have called you friends, for all things that I heard from My Father I have made known to you. John 15:15

Nevertheless when one turns to the Lord, the veil is taken away. II Corinthians 5:16

There is no more separation. The veil has been removed. Christ is in you and you are in Him. You are empowered by His Spirit and equipped with His mind. The hidden things of God are made known through discernment and divine revelation. You are a friend of God, and He doesn't keep secrets from His friends.

[9] But as it is written: "Eye has not seen, nor ear heard, nor have entered into the heart of man the things which God prepared for those who love Him. [10] But God has revealed them to us through His Spirit. For the Spirit searches all things, yes, the deep things of God. [11] For what man knows the things of a man except the spirit of the man which is in him? Even so no one knows the things of God except the Spirit of God. [12] Now we have received, not the spirit of the world, but the Spirit who is from God, that we might know the things that have been freely given to us by God. I Corinthians 2:9-12

There is more to you than the past has shown. Preparation was made for you before time began. Despite previous pain and heartache, you were created on purpose for a purpose. This journey was meant for now. See with God's eyes. Hear with His ears, love with His heart, and speak His Word to see the manifestation of the reality He preordained for you. Call heaven's reality to earth by faith.

Commit to living out the Word daily. Will it be easy? No, not always. This is a different reality. Perfection isn't a priority; availability is. The race won't always won by the swift or the battle by the strong; endurance is the key to this promised victory. Life has never been nor will it ever be a cake walk, but in this new reality, triumph is guaranteed. Trials will come. That's okay. The ability to overcome has been imparted to you. Glean from the words of Jesus. *These things I have spoken to you, that in Me you may have peace. In the world you will have tribulation; but be of good cheer, I have overcome the world."* (John 16:33). Christ has already defeated EVERY battle you will ever face. EVER! Embrace that assurance. This journey is not for the faint at heart. Through every fire and in every valley, I urge you to look to the Spirit of God as your Comforter. His joy is your strength. (Nehemiah 8:10). Continue to draw near to Him.

FACT: You have unlimited access to the great I AM. Savior, Lord, Friend, Comforter, Deliverer, Protector – the list goes on. Everything you need, He is. Seek His face. Find rest in His presence. Press In. Commit this verse to memory:

But seek first the kingdom of God and His righteousness, and all these things shall be added unto you. Matthew 6:33

Focus upward. Lean in to hear.

⁵ Trust in the Lord with all your heart, and lean not on your own understanding. ⁶ In all your ways acknowledge Him, and He shall direct your paths. Proverbs 3:5-6

Four times the Scriptures state, "The just shall live by faith." You are the just. Trust in the Lord. Walk as the Spirit of God leads.

¹⁹ Therefore, brethren, having boldness to enter the Holiest by the blood of Jesus, ²⁰ by a new and living way which He consecrated for us, through the veil, that is, His flesh, ²¹ and having a High Priest over the house of God, ²² let us draw near with a true heart in full assurance of faith, having our hearts sprinkled from an evil conscience and our bodies washed with pure water. ²³ Let us hold fast the confession of our hope without wavering, for He who promised is faithful. Hebrews 10:19-23

You are not your past. Newness in Christ is yours! So what if others accuse you of acting brand new?!?!? You are! The old has passed away; the true you has made its debut. You now know who you are because you know WHOSE you are. Ayyye! The past is behind you. Begin speaking of things to come. Passion, purpose, and promises are attached to you. A fulfilling future is destined for you!

Once broken, the Father has healed you. Once rejected and neglected, He marks you as loved and accepted. When He calls for you to seek His face, be like David and sincerely respond, "Your face, Lord, I will seek." (Psalm 27:8).

You have access into the presence of the King of Kings. Abide there. Listen upward. Press in. Move forward and trust fully. Go deeper... in Christ. Love God without restraint – no limits, boundaries, or distrust. This is the will of the Lord for your life. He who calls you is faithful. His love will never disappoint. Go forth and bear much fruit... in the name of Jesus.

14 The sower sows the word. 15 And these are the ones by the wayside where the word is sown. When they hear, Satan comes immediately and takes away the word that was sown in their hearts. 16 These likewise are the ones sown on stony ground who, when they hear the word, immediately receive it with gladness; [17] and they have no root in themselves, and so endure only for a time. Afterward, when tribulation or persecution arises for the word's sake, immediately they stumble. [18] Now these are the ones sown among thorns; they are the ones who hear the word, [19] and the cares of this world, the deceitfulness of riches, and the desires for other things entering in choke the word, and it becomes unfruitful. [20] But these are the ones sown on good ground, those who hear the word, accept it, and bear fruit: some thirtyfold, some sixty, and some a hundred." Mark 4:14-20

Dear Lord,

You are the Vine; this precious daughter is Your branch. You will not fail at the work You began. Cultivate her heart and mind according to Your truth. Shape her according to Your perfect will. Give her eyes to see the masterpiece You fashioned her to be.

Thank You for being her Father, Friend, Comforter, and Peace. She stands because You are her strength. She overcomes because You are her victory. Lord, it is in You that she lives, moves, and has her being. Continue to increase her faith in the validity of Your Word. Help her to know You more fully and trust You more deeply. There is no wavering in Your character. Help her to trust in Your faithfulness.

Thank You for speaking to her heart. This isn't the end of her journey; it is merely the beginning of a new season of freedom. Holy Spirit, guide her steps. Make the way plain. In Jesus' holy name I pray. Amen.

Listen Up: Thoughts of Revival

Home is where the heart is, and your heart is safely secured in the hands of the Father. The space below is yours to reflect on your journey of healing and revival.

About the Author

LaToya NaShae's passion and purpose are equipping others to live like they know WHOSE they are. This is accomplished through the avenues of writing, speaking, and coaching.

She readily comes along beside others on their journey to discovering who they are in Christ and becoming empowered to walk in purpose. Whether publicly declaring the Good News of Christ or engaged in one-on-one coaching, LaToya walks with others along their journey of faith and freedom. Her aim is to encourage others to become unstuck in their minds, unbound in their lives, and unbreakable in their Christ-identity.

LaToya NaShae is a graduate of Murray State University and the Christian Coach Institute. She currently resides in Middle Tennessee where she serves as the founder and lead coach of BREAKOUT Coaching.

Connect with LaToya NaShae

Facebook: Breakout-Coaching

Instagram: @coach_latoyanashae

YouTube: LaToya NaShae

www.ingramcontent.com/pod-product-compliance
Lightning Source LLC
Chambersburg PA
CBHW060016050426
42448CB00012B/2773